PATRICK WILSON

AMERINGER
McENERY
YOHE

525 West 22nd Street New York NY 10011
tel 212 445 0051 www.amy-nyc.com

WAYS OF SEEING

By Lilly Wei

When I asked Patrick Wilson how his newest body of work might have changed, he responded that change isn't something he consciously thinks about. Whatever changes occur—and changes are inevitable—are organic, process-based, and dictated by the painting as it progresses from a state of becoming into being, into an object made up of specific resolutions. Substantive changes in his production can't be forced, he said, and they are more evident across time spans of perhaps five or ten years.

That noted, his recent paintings seem, nonetheless, to be moving toward a greater complexity. Formats and compositions are more variable—although they remain unwaveringly rectilinear in structure—and colors are even more breathtaking and nuanced, the juxtapositions often quirky and unpredictable. Their spatial dynamics are increasingly enigmatic and baroque, the orientation at times emphatically vertical, as with *Chef* and *Dreamer* (both 2016), or horizontal, as with *Pool House, Garden House,* and *Cliff House* (all 2016), but still bespoke, based on his body's measurements. Throughout his career, Wilson has been an artist who is in his studio virtually every day, simply as a way of life.

Wilson, a Los Angeles-based painter who received his BA from the University of California, Davis, and has an MFA from Claremont Graduate University, was raised on West Coast Minimalism, which includes movements such as Hard-Edge, Light and Space, and Finish Fetish, with perhaps a hint of Op Art thrown in. Artists whose works have been crucial to Wilson's evolution include

John McLaughlin, Frederick Hammersley, Helen Lundeberg, John McCracken, Larry Bell, Richard Diebenkorn, and Robert Irwin, as well as Ken Price, George Nakashima, and the mid-century Swedish textile artist Märta Måås-Fjetterström and others in her workshop.

Materiality is central to his practice, and he is fastidious about his choices. An accomplished craftsman, his surfaces are constructed by hand, using tape and a drywall blade to pull the pigment across. But they are immaculate, as if they had been industrially planed and polished. That improbable perfection is one of their most striking qualities, a trompe-l'oeil of facture that is only one of a number of visual feints he deploys to tantalize and engage the viewer.

Wilson comes from a creative family that has always supported his endeavors. His father, a painter, has been a great influence, as has his mother and his grandfather, both designers. Another influence is location. His work—like that of many of the artists he gravitates toward—is steeped in the landscape of Southern California, reflecting both its reality and mythos. It is a place where sky, sea, and light can be stunning, but also harsh, situated at land's end, the urbanized and the natural in exultant but uneasy proximity.

Wilson addresses that codependency by means of hard-edged square and rectangular planes in a spectrum of subtle, poetic, and dimensional colors that soften and disrupt the literalness of geometric shape. Some forms are opaque, others translucent, absorbing and reflecting the ambient light; at times, the paintings look as if they are uncannily illuminated from within. A superb colorist (who discriminatingly shoehorns color in at every opportunity), he tilts his hues toward the indescribable, the unnameable. White, grey, and celadon, for instance, as he interprets them, become a light rather than a single color note, shifting as you look at them. And even his more standard choices, say, a bold block of green or brilliant red, a bar of deep blue, can turn elusive, built up from multiple shades.

The grids that divide his paintings often suggest façades or other architectural constructs. They also recall the windows that have framed the pictorial world throughout much of the history of Western painting, the portal between reality and illusion. Wilson's frames, however, are contemporary, and they displace, question. He derails expectation and complacency, requiring a more complicit, active gaze. Pitting geometry against color, he orchestrates dissonances that are held in check, reconciled but bracing. It is the tension that results when line contends with color, flatness with spatial indeterminacy, and factuality with aura, the beat of coloristic advance and retreat adding further vibrancy and breath.

In his early years as a painter, his work depicted real objects as anchors of sorts, but by now he has eliminated all such references, trusting to the experiential and the optical, to the satisfactions of color, form, texture, and light. He works, for the most part, without preliminary studies, letting the painting's progress take him to completion. That means he is constantly adjusting, like a surfer riding a wave, reacting to what he has just done, righting missteps, shifting directions, and rebalancing. He says he finds "failures" to be "productive, even necessary, for the growth of the painting." And, in another visual feint, he creates a trompe-l'oeil of material, one that has an extra spin. What might look like an assemblage of the thinnest sheets of overlaid tinted plastic, are in actuality layers and layers of acrylic paint. Some planes are slightly raised, the built-up paint suggesting plastic micro-stacks, which in essence they are, since acrylic is plastic, as Wilson points out, adroitly converting deception into truth.

While there is much more than figure/ground relationships in Wilson's paintings, they are critical to his repertory, part of the visual conundrum he creates, the illusions he spins, and the deceptions he explores and purposely complicates. Are the topmost forms overlaid over multiple others beneath them, or are the forms that seem to be situated underneath simply bands in some instances, edging the surface planes? Are some planes located within and over others, or are they meant to be a shadow, a reflection of what is behind or below? What is foregrounded? What is in the middle ground, in the background? Lines add their own colors to the composition, lines that might suddenly terminate or change hue, interrupting the reading—the rectangle or square outlined (or overlaid by a transparent form?) and perhaps no longer defined quite as you had thought nor situated where you had thought. He messes with us, but that's more than fine.

Martini (2016) and *Tansu* (2016) are two exemplary recent ventures. The titles are personal and associative and have little, if anything, to do with the compositions beyond that. *Martini*, at first glance a relatively pale painting, although chock full of colors, amusingly suggests a cool, heady drink, and *Tansu*, more esoteric, refers to Japanese wooden cabinets, sometimes lacquered, with their cunningly arranged drawers, evoked, no doubt, by the structure of the painting. Another, *Sommelier* (2016), regales us with jeweled colors that recall those of rare red wines and, if you unleash the sensorium of your imagination, perhaps even a whiff of wine's seductive bouquet. But like many artists who work abstractly, Wilson feels it is important that interpretations remain open and that viewers make their own associations.

Martini is cooler, lower-keyed, and *Tansu* is warmer, higher-pitched. The latter is dominated by a ravishing red, next to which is a mercurial, difficult-to-pinpoint shade that might be likened to the pearlescent light of dawn. Each is carefully balanced between cool and warm, translucent and matte, silken and slightly rough—as are all of his paintings, which must be seen in actuality. Their details, their souls, are lost in reproductions, in which they become flat and graphic. Nothing can quite capture the exquisite tonalities of the color, or the creaminess of the acrylic, which is as luxurious as oil paint, or the slight unevenness of the surface topography. The paint also extends beyond the support to form a band around its edges, not visible from a frontal view, imposing another frame of sorts. It extends no more than a quarter inch or so, but it is enough to emphasize the work's physicality, its materiality. Yet the slight halo of reflected color that emanates from it, depending on the available light, can have an opposite effect, questioning the discreteness of the surface and where it actually ends, leading the work, once again, away from certainties.

Wilson offers an alternative to the rapid scan that characterizes the way many of us, inundated with the ceaseless stream of imagery blasted across numerous platforms, now look at artwork. His works require and reward a slower read, challenging the viewer to go on a perceptual treasure hunt, to look more attentively, more deeply. They brim with small, unexpected flourishes and insertions—a dash of color here, a seepage or blush or bloom there, a hue that appears nowhere else in the particular painting, and much more—tucked into corners, into edges, into the interstitial spaces between planes, wherever an accent or a further line adjustment might be needed. If the colors were named, they might not seem so varied or arresting, since precise identifying words for hues are limited ("red," for instance, does not distinguish all the reds he confects and conjures); to the eye, however, his palette is infinitely richer.

What ultimately stands out for me is the tribute that Wilson pays to the eye's discernment and to the miraculous powers of the artist's hand and touch. His insistence on formal beauty as an attribute of redemptive, humanistic value, something to be desired and pursued, is compelling. While such art has, at times, been considered elitist or disengaged from political and social realities, it might also be considered activist, bestowing its own significant gifts on us. Not the least of these gifts is a sense of possibility—and of grace.　■

Lilly Wei is a New York-based independent curator and critic whose focus is contemporary art. She has written regularly for *Art in America* since 1984, and she is a contributing editor at *ARTnews*. Wei has also written for *Art + Australia, Asian Art News, Sanat Dünyamiz, Art Papers, Sculpture* magazine, *Tema Celeste, Flash Art, Art Press,* and *Art + Auction,* among other publications. She has been the author of numerous exhibition catalogues on contemporary art, including publications for the Albright-Knox Art Gallery in Buffalo, NY; the Neuberger Museum of Art in Purchase, NY; and the Metropolitan Museum of Art in New York City. Wei was born in Chengdu, China, and has a master's degree in art history from Columbia University.

Improvise, 2016
Acrylic on canvas
22 x 22 inches
55.9 x 55.9 cm

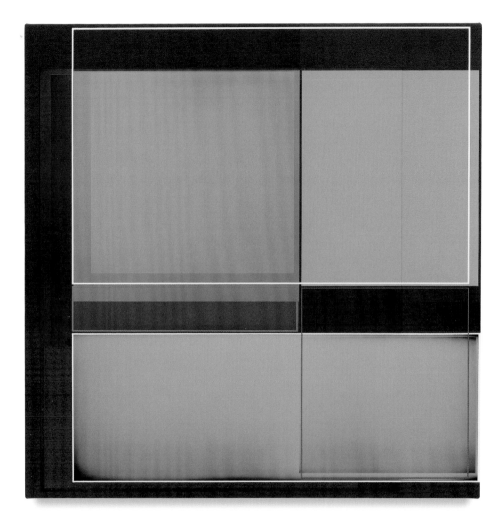

Build, 2016
Acrylic on canvas
22 x 22 inches
55.9 x 55.9 cm

Slice, 2016
Acrylic on canvas
22 x 22 inches
55.9 x 55.9 cm

Stack, 2016
Acrylic on canvas
22 x 22 inches
55.9 x 55.9 cm

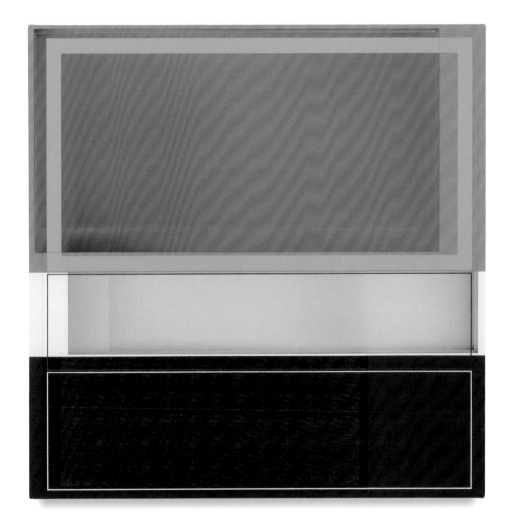

Draw, 2016
Acrylic on canvas
22 x 22 inches
55.9 x 55.9 cm

Rotate, 2016
Acrylic on canvas
22 x 22 inches
55.9 x 55.9 cm

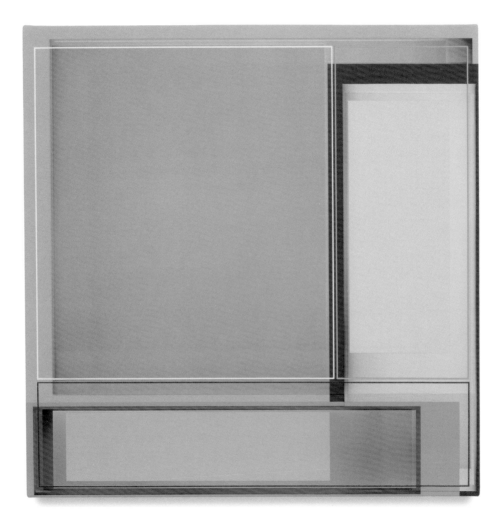

Desert House (for Divola), 2016
Acrylic on canvas
30 x 72 inches
76.2 x 182.9 cm

Garden House, 2016
Acrylic on canvas
30 x 72 inches
76.2 x 182.9 cm

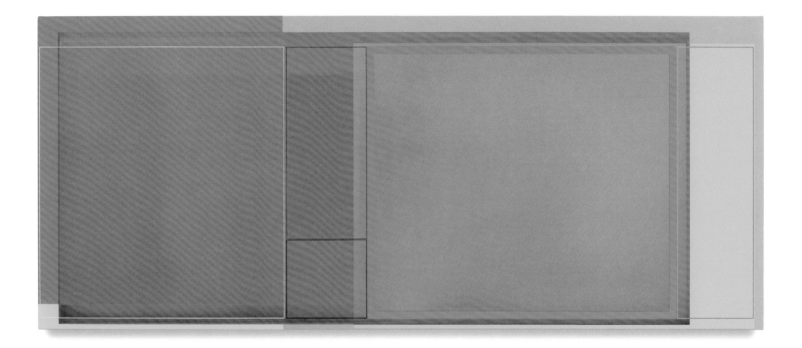

Pool House, 2016
Acrylic on canvas
30 x 72 inches
76.2 x 182.9 cm

Cliff House, 2016
Acrylic on canvas
30 x 72 inches
76.2 x 182.9 cm

Tansu, 2016
Acrylic on canvas
59 x 49 inches
149.9 x 124.5 cm

At Sundown, 2016
Acrylic on canvas
59 x 49 inches
149.9 x 124.5 cm

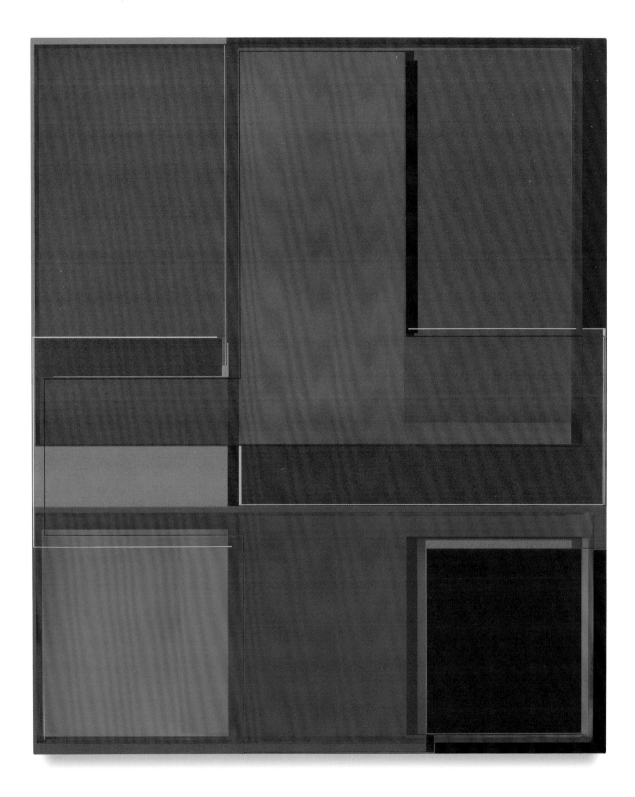

Martini, 2016
Acrylic on canvas
59 x 49 inches
149.9 x 124.5 cm

On the Bay, 2016
Acrylic on canvas
59 x 49 inches
149.9 x 124.5 cm

Mississippi Blue Cat, 2016
Acrylic on canvas
59 x 49 inches
149.9 x 124.5 cm

Rock Garden, 2016
Acrylic on canvas
59 x 49 inches
149.9 x 124.5 cm

Sommelier, 2016
Acrylic on canvas
86 x 39 inches
218.4 x 99.1 cm

Diva, 2016
Acrylic on canvas
86 x 39 inches
218.4 x 99.1 cm

Dreamer, 2016
Acrylic on canvas
86 x 39 inches
218.4 x 99.1 cm

Chef, 2016
Acrylic on canvas
86 x 39 inches
218.4 x 99.1 cm

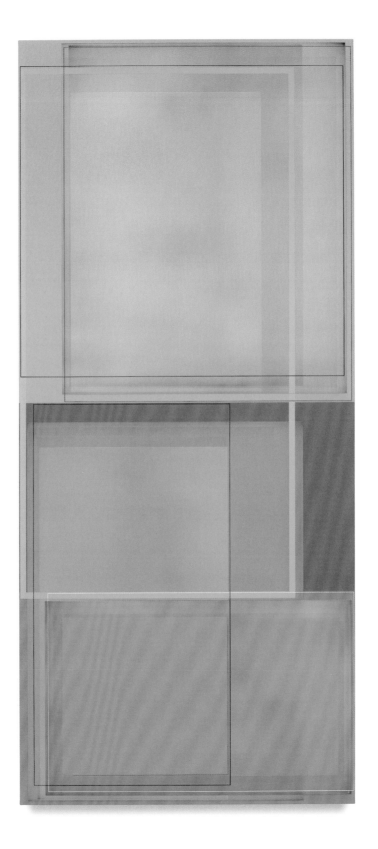

Daredevil, 2016
Acrylic on canvas
86 x 39 inches
218.4 x 99.1 cm

Philosopher, 2016
Acrylic on canvas
86 x 39 inches
218.4 x 99.1 cm

Fieldwork, 2016
Acrylic on canvas
70 x 86 inches
177.8 x 218.4 cm

Time, 2016
Acrylic on canvas
70 x 86 inches
177.8 x 218.4 cm

Long Walk, 2016
Acrylic on canvas
15 x 36 inches
38.1 x 91.4 cm

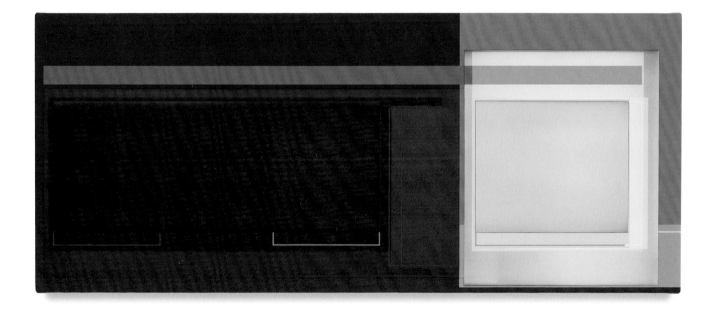

Funhouse, 2016
Acrylic on canvas
15 x 36 inches
38.1 x 91.4 cm

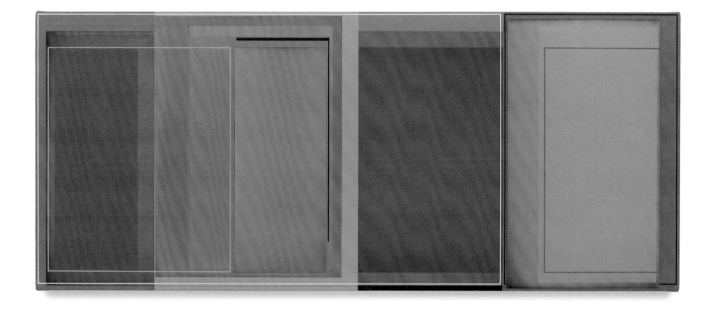

Music House (for Sonny Clark), 2016
Acrylic on canvas
15 x 36 inches
38.1 x 91.4 cm

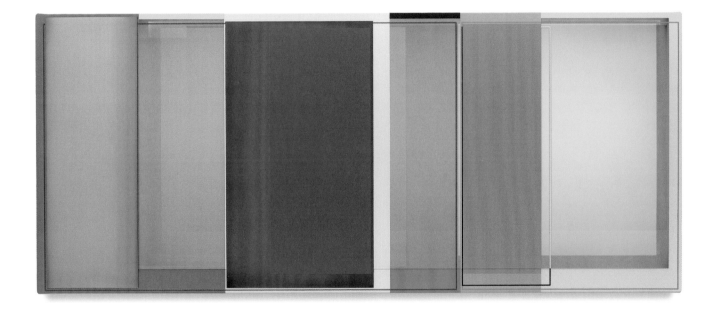

The Storm, 2016
Acrylic on canvas
15 x 36 inches
38.1 x 91.4 cm

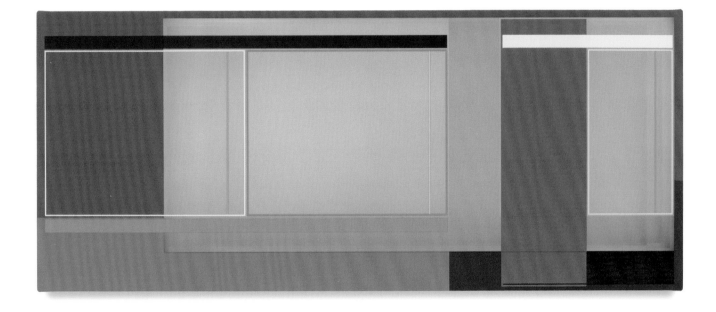

By The River, 2016
Acrylic on canvas
15 x 36 inches
38.1 x 91.4 cm

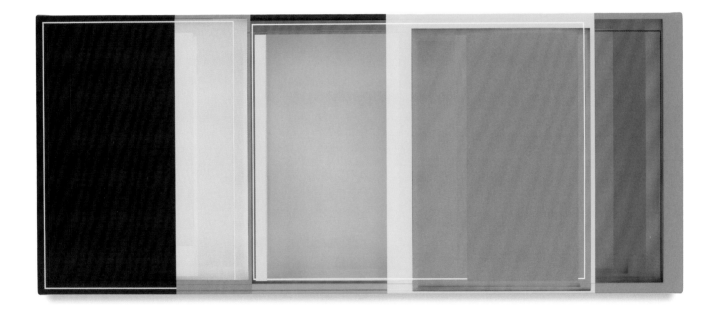

The Calm, 2016
Acrylic on canvas
15 x 36 inches
38.1 x 91.4 cm

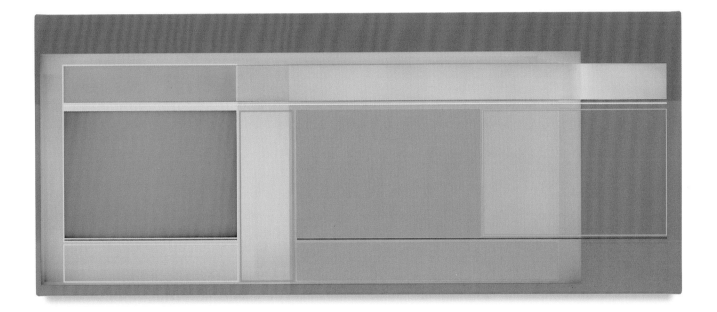

Published on the occasion of the exhibition

PATRICK WILSON

27 April – 26 May 2017

Ameringer | McEnery | Yohe
525 West 22nd Street
New York, NY 10011
tel 212 445 0051
www.amy-nyc.com

Artwork photography by
Robert Wedemeyer, Los Angeles, CA

Cover and installation photography by
Christopher Burke Studios, New York, NY

Catalogue designed by
HHA Design, New York, NY

ISBN: 978-0-9979454-4-7

Cover: *Time* (detail), 2016